BASKETBALL HALL OF FAMERS

WILT CHAMBERLAIN

Robert Greenberger

Published in 2002 by The Rosen Publishing Group, Inc.
29 East 21st Street, New York, NY 10010

Library of Congress Cataloging-in-Publication Data

Greenberger, Robert.
Wilt Chamberlain / by Robert Greenberger.
p. cm. — (Basketball Hall of Famers)
Includes bibliographical references and index.
ISBN 0-8239-3486-1 (lib. bdg.)
1. Chamberlain, Wilt, 1936– —Juvenile literature. 2. Basketball
players—United States—Biography—Juvenile literature. 3. African
American basketball players—Biography—Juvenile literature.
[1. Chamberlain, Wilt, 1936– 2. Basketball players. 3. African
Americans—Biography.] I. Title. II. Series.
GV884.C5 G74 2002
796.323'092—dc21

2001003454

Manufactured in the United States of America

contents

In every sport there are players who help shape and redefine the game. These players become legends, their feats remembered, and have names that live on throughout sports history. Within the world of professional basketball, one such man is Wilt Chamberlain.

He brought national attention to a game that was almost never televised and rarely spoken about between fans. People looked up in awe as this seven-foot-one-inch athlete took the court and made magic happen. His name remains atop almost every record in the sport, and his style of play inspired generation after generation of athletes. Chamberlain literally *rewrote* the rules—they were altered to accommodate a player of his size and caliber.

With his size, strength, quickness, and a determination to score and rebound at will, Wilt Chamberlain became the greatest offensive player in the history of professional basketball.

He was a new breed of superstar who dominated the game during each of his fourteen seasons. Chamberlain went on to become a larger-than-life figure who always seemed to be doing something—usually for someone else.

From his lower middle-class beginnings in Philadelphia, Pennsylvania, he played with passion and he was determined to excel. He also made sure to achieve his goals. His many accomplishments are the makings of myth. His 100-point game and his rivalry with Boston Celtics' center Bill Russell for instance, rank with the greatest competitors in any sport.

"No one ever roots for Goliath," was something Wilt Chamberlain always said about his relationship with the fans. But he never stopped to hear the cheering; he just played the game. Chamberlain was intelligent enough to know when he needed to make adjustments or learn new skills. He proved this while twice helping to bring his team to the national championship.

Introduction

When he died in 1999 at age sixty-three, the accolades from teammates, journalists, spectators, and even former rivals all saluted his status as a great man and athlete. His accomplishments, both on and off the court built that reputation, making him an admired man even after his death.

A Star Grows in Philadelphia

When Wilton Norman was born into the Chamberlain family, he was just another member of a growing clan that ultimately totaled nine children: six boys and three girls. Wilton was born on August 21, 1936, during the Great Depression, but his father, William, always managed to find work, keeping the family sheltered and safe. William held a variety of jobs, including shipyard welder and handyman at Sears department store, while his wife, Olivia, raised the family. She was an excellent cook, keeping hot dishes on the table for everyone to enjoy.

Chamberlain recalled his father taking the time to bring him to sporting events from an early age, showing him what someone can do given enough drive and perseverance. Young Chamberlain recognized his father's efforts to teach him athletic discipline. As an adult, he said his parents were the best teachers he ever had.

West Philadelphia was a safe and loving environment for the young sports enthusiast. When they could afford it, the Chamberlains moved into a house and the girls began taking piano lessons. Chamberlain and his brothers played a variety of sports on the streets. Still, he was conscious that the family was always careful with their money. His mother, who before the move almost always remained at home, began cleaning houses to help meet monthly expenses.

An Awkward Youth

Even as a child, Chamberlain was taller than his friends. He felt older as a result of his enormous growth, and saw the need to help his family make ends meet. At seven years of age, he began helping the local milkman lift and stack crates. Olivia was pleased that her son wanted to help the family, but told the milkman that the boy was too young to work. The astonished man had thought Chamberlain was at least five years older given his size and strength.

All the Chamberlain children attended public school including Wilt who, by the time he finished elementary school, was already more than six feet tall. That summer, he visited his uncle's farm in Virginia and helped work the fields. The mixture of sun, fresh air, and hard work added six more inches to his height by the time he returned home.

As a junior high school student, Chamberlain played basketball, recognizing that his size gave him advantages. He soon stopped playing other popular sports such as stickball and football, and concentrated mainly on basketball. He played for any team that would have him, including the Police Athletic League, church teams, and the local YMCA.

Although he excelled in sports thanks to his nearly seven-foot frame, he remained self-conscious about his size while away from the

Basketball: An American Game

Basketball, recognized as the first truly American sport, was created in the nineteenth century. Dr. James Naismith, a Canadian-born physical education instructor, developed the game while at the International YMCA Training School (now known as Springfield College). Responsible for the physical education program, he recognized that the winter months made it difficult for the students to do anything challenging indoors. Starting with a leather soccer ball, Naismith suggested it to be thrown into boxes. But without any nearby, he instructed the custodians to nail peach baskets at each end of the gymnasium instead, giving the game its name. The sport has changed little since 1891. The fruit baskets, eventually replaced by hoops and a backboard, were ten feet from the ground, the same distance as in today's games. Originally he had nine players per side, but in short order the number was reduced to five.

Dr. James Naismith

The Basketball Hall of Fame in Springfield, Massachusetts

With only thirteen rules to guide the competition, basketball's popularity quickly developed. Within a year, the game was adopted for use at other schools, notably Vassar College and Smith College for women. In fact, when the first women played the game, Maude Sherman played so well that Naismith was captivated. Later, they married.

By 1898, the first professional teams played for the National Basketball League, and Naismith's dream brought him fame.

Since the birthplace of basketball was Springfield, Massachusetts, it is fitting that the Basketball Hall of Fame, founded in 1959, now resides there.

courts. Chamberlain was teased throughout his entire life because of his size, but his young peers were especially cruel. "You learn to tolerate [verbal abuse], but I do not know whether you ever fully accept it or not," he explained years later. He was embarrassed to put on his playing shorts since he had such long, thin legs. And although his parents taught him to give women his seat on the subway, he stopped doing so because of the looks he received whenever he stood up. He was often mistaken for being older; for example, he was often asked to pay adult prices at the movies when he was still a minor.

Chamberlain was also shy because of a persistent stutter that he managed to correct over the years. However, little in the way of self-doubt affected his schoolwork. Chamberlain never neglected his studies. He displayed a keen mind for many different subjects, absorbing all he could.

High School Hero

While attending Philadelphia's Overbrook High School, Chamberlain became a statewide star who led his team to victory after victory. He attracted much attention, and sports reporters began covering his games. *Philadelphia Bulletin* reporter Jack Ryan gave him the notorious nickname "Wilt the Stilt."

Wilt hated that nickname, although people used it for his entire life. To his closest friends he was "Big Norman," and by most others he preferred to be called "The Big Dipper." That nickname was given to Chamberlain because he had to constantly "dip" his head to avoid doorways, lights, and branches. As the story goes, he earned the moniker when, while playing basketball in the basement of an abandoned house, he hit his head on a low-hanging pipe.

At seventeen, Wilt Chamberlain was a member of Overbrook High's track-and-field team and the school's basketball star.

The high school coach helped young Chamberlain win games by having his teammates miss their free throws, allowing him to grab the rebounds and repeatedly toss in baskets. On the other hand, showing a small streak of selfishness, Chamberlain also helped to tip balls into the hoop even though they were going in anyway. This was called goaltending and is currently illegal in both college and professional play.

By the end of his high school career, Chamberlain's team had lost a mere three times and he had shattered state scoring records for high school play. In fact, twice he scored a total of 90 points during a game, which was unheard of in the 1950s.

Chamberlain did not rely entirely on his height to achieve fame—he also worked out, developing his muscle tone and coordination. He was one of the earliest ball players to lift weights. During the summers, he would find his way into gyms and spend hours working on his jump shots, honing the skills he would need during the following season.

Chamberlain Gets Drafted

As a born athlete, Chamberlain also loved track. He spent his time running and became a track star, too, thanks again to those long, powerful legs. His first experiences with athletics were on the track field, as a runner for the Pennsylvania Relays. He also excelled at field events such as the javelin toss.

As expected, his exploits garnered the attention of scouts from colleges across the United States. Although the number has varied in the retelling, it's safe to say that well over 100 colleges wanted Chamberlain to come play on their teams. He even went to see a dozen schools, keeping each trip a secret to avoid speculation from the press.

At the same time, Eddie Gottlieb, the owner of the Philadelphia Warriors, had plans of his own for Chamberlain. The Warriors were a part of the National Basketball Association (NBA), the major professional league. In those days, the rules allowed owners to draft players within their territory to help keep local audiences interested in the still-growing league.

Gottlieb convinced his fellow league owners to let him draft Chamberlain as his territorial draft pick, even though the rules said that high school students couldn't be drafted. "Why not," he said at the time. "Listen, I guarantee that [Wilt] Chamberlain will be our

Eddie Gottlieb, president and coach of the Philadelphia Warriors in 1952

first-round pick after his senior year in college and I'm taking him now. If he breaks a leg, if he can't play—I still get him. I'm taking a gamble on the guy."

During the summer between high school and college, Chamberlain worked as a bellman at Kutsher's Country Club in the Catskill Mountains. He played on a small team coached by the famous Red Auerbach, who tried to

The NBA

P laying basketball as a career came about fairly quickly after it was established as a college sport. Of the original teams in the National Basketball League, the best-remembered team was the original Boston Celtics, known for their terrific team play.

There were a variety of leagues formed, similar to the growth of professional baseball, but none seemed to capture the public's imagination like the American and National Leagues did at the turn of the century.

The National Basketball Association was formed in 1949, when the Basketball Association of America and the National Basketball League merged into one new group. They began with seventeen teams, with center George Mikan, the best-known player in the league.

As the NBA, they carefully cultivated players, allowing teams to draft regionally so college stars could continue playing for the hometown audiences. It wasn't until the point-shaving scandal of 1950 that local players became national stars. Bob Cousy and Bob Petit joined Mikan as early NBA standouts. In 1956, Bill Russell began playing, making the new Celtics a dynasty, much as the Yankees dominated baseball. By the time Chamberlain arrived, basketball took its place as one of America's premier sports.

convince him to attend Harvard University so the Boston Celtics could challenge the territorial pick. Chamberlain, being so tall, teamed with another bellman, and, as a service to second-floor guests, would bring their luggage to the window. He'd place the bags on his head and the other bellman would lean out the second-story window and haul them into the room. This proved faster than routine methods, and the two made extra tip money.

To protect his territorial pick, Gottlieb helped to influence Chamberlain's college choice: the University of Kansas. Since no NBA franchise was in the area, none could counter the claim. This also kept Chamberlain from attending local Pennsylvania schools that would draw potential audiences away from the Warriors—shrewd thinking on Gottlieb's part. It was also in the middle of the country and seen as a quiet place for Chamberlain to continue perfecting his game while managing to complete his studies.

3

Hidden Away in Kansas

Now that he was playing for his college coach Phog Allen, Chamberlain refined his game. He finally stopped growing at seven feet one inch, and could start adding additional muscle to his athletic frame. He also continued with his track work and tied for first place in the high jump during an eight-school competition.

But Chamberlain saw another side to life away from home, and it bothered him. Despite his African American friends who assured him he would be treated well at the school, Chamberlain was more than a little rattled to learn that the University of Kansas was segregated, which meant there were separate

Wilt Chamberlain stands with his University of Kansas teammates after winning the Big Seven Conference Invitational Tournament on December 29, 1957.

facilities for black and white students. Race had not been an issue for Chamberlain in the past, but he could not help noticing that it was an issue that concerned the entire nation.

During the 1950s, segregation was one of the biggest problems facing the country. The Supreme Court had ruled that separate-but-equal facilities were illegal in the landmark decision *Brown v. Board of Education of Topeka*, but integration was slow to spread across the nation because people were resistant to change.

"I was a brash young man of color coming into a white societal sport and taking over—commanding and demanding. Do you think I was liked for that?" Chamberlain told a reporter for the *Kansas City Star*. "I don't think so." Southern Methodist fans sang "Bye-Bye Blackbird" when he once fouled out of a game, a pointed reference to his color.

Dr. Franklin Murphy, president of the university, was ahead of his peers in wanting to encourage blacks and whites to coexist in harmony. This helped to smooth things for Chamberlain during his college years. The college saw other firsts, too. Upon Chamberlain's arrival, a special oversized bed was ordered for the dormitory where he would reside.

He studied business and foreign languages, excelling in his coursework as well as on the basketball court. He was well liked and quickly joined one of the black fraternities on campus.

24 Wilt Chamberlain, seven-foot-one center for the University of Kansas basketball team, gears up for a game.

A Kansas City Superstar

Playing for the Kansas City Jayhawks, Chamberlain continued to post impressive scoring records, but he was also subjected to national media scrutiny anytime the team lost. Even though he was one of five players on the court, he was the tallest, the fastest, and the strongest of them and it was assumed he would personally win each contest. The media pressure was intense even during his freshman year, when university rules forced him to play junior varsity (JV). There was no JV schedule so the team scrimmaged (practiced) against the varsity team, prepping Chamberlain for his place among the more experienced players.

During his tenure with the varsity team, he did help them reach the National College Athletic Association's (NCAA) championship game. In what many consider the finest college basketball game of all time, the Jayhawks and the North Carolina Wolfpack matched each other point for point. The game went beyond the buzzer and ended with a triple overtime. To the end of his days, Chamberlain said the Jayhawks' one-point loss was one of the most crushing defeats of his life.

Despite an average of 29.9 points and 18.3 rebounds per game, Chamberlain was restless after his junior year and dissatisfied with the University of Kansas. Opportunities for his basketball prowess were available and he was ready. The NBA rules prevented Gottlieb from signing Chamberlain as a junior, although the Warriors owner tried.

The Ultimate Dream

Instead, Chamberlain signed with the most famous basketball team of them all, the Harlem Globetrotters.

Before African Americans played regularly in the professional leagues, Abe Saperstein's Harlem Globetrotters traveled the world. They barnstormed (toured) from one end of the United States to the other, and then went through other countries, sometimes playing as many as three games per day. The finest black basketball players were with the

Globies, who were respected not only for their athleticism, but also for their ability to entertain the masses.

How much the team paid Chamberlain has remained a mystery, although reports estimate that his salary ranged from $50,000 to $65,000 a year. Chamberlain claimed to have turned down $100,000 a year from a rival group, the Harlem Wizards, before accepting the Globetrotter offer. Whatever the figure, it allowed him to buy his parents a newer, larger home.

"When I was a young boy first learning the game of basketball," Chamberlain wrote in his autobiography, *A View from Above*, "the ultimate dream for players of color was to play with the Globetrotters. The NBA meant zero to us at that time. In my eyes, and in the eyes of many others, they were the best basketball team in the world. To be that good and that funny, what could be more desirable?"

Chamberlain, who had studied languages in college, loved being exposed to European cities and cultures. He also noted that being

Wilt Chamberlain poses with Abe Saperstein, owner and coach of the Harlem Globetrotters, shortly after signing with the team in 1958.

black in Europe was not as much of an obstacle as it was in the United States. It was a thrilling year that did more to educate him than his senior year at the University of Kansas ever would have. In fact, he was on the team in 1958, when the Globetrotters played their first-ever game in the Soviet city of Moscow.

The Globetrotters often played on a double bill with NBA teams to boost attendance, so Chamberlain was exposed to the men who would later be his teammates and rivals.

His year-long experience made him a better player, but he turned down offers to continue. It was time for his professional debut. With the support of Eddie Gottlieb, Chamberlain signed a $30,000 contract with the Philadelphia Warriors and finally joined the NBA.

Finally in the NBA

Chamberlain's friends and peers warned him that playing in the professional league would be difficult. In fact, they told him that other players were going to go after him because of his height and fame. But hearing those words was much different from actually enduring the physical abuse that professional play would bring.

Chamberlain burst into the NBA in the fall of 1959 and was an immediate rookie sensation. People flocked to see the Philadelphia Warriors compete, and Chamberlain scored point after point. The National Broadcasting Company (NBC), the television network that usually broadcast a single weekly basketball game every Sunday afternoon, added a Saturday broadcast to cover Chamberlain better. By the end of his first season, Chamberlain rewrote the record books in most scoring categories. His 37.6 points-per-game average was a full 30 percent ahead of the previous record. And although he appreciated the crowds and loved playing, the other teams initially jostled him because of his record-breaking talent. In 1962 he recalled, "This is a rough game. I didn't expect as much shoving and holding and pushing. But I can't say I wasn't warned. They told me I'd be a target for everyone in the league and I am."

The same frustration was seen in his play. Sometimes he grabbed a rebound with one massive hand and, instead of passing it to his teammates, smacked it against the other hand. This created a sound loud enough to rattle the smaller players near him. On blocked shots, he swatted violently at the ball, more often than not knocking it out of bounds, giving the opposing team another chance. This was quite often the result of match-ups against centers who were near his height.

Coach Neil Johnston was unsure of how to handle Chamberlain and uncertain of how best to

Philadelphia Warrior Wilt Chamberlain dunks to score his 3,000th point of the 1961–1962 season in Syracuse, New York, on February 8, 1962. He would go on to score 4,029 points that season, a new NBA record.

channel his playing style for the good of the team. He and Chamberlain clashed on more than one occasion, making that first year emotionally difficult for the rookie player. Complicating the relationship was the fact that Chamberlain was Johnston's replacement on the team; it was the former center's first coaching assignment. Johnston's inexperience made Chamberlain's introduction to the world of professional basketball extremely unpleasant. Additionally, from Chamberlain's perspective, Johnston was another in a long line of coaches who told him how to play when it was clear he just needed to relax.

Chamberlain Meets Russell

That first year also saw the start of a rivalry between Chamberlain and Boston Celtics center Bill Russell. The all-star player with the number six jersey had debuted two years earlier and had helped propel the Celtics to an unparalleled run of championships. The two centers faced off time and again, with Russell usually outplaying number thirteen (although Chamberlain did manage many more rebounds than any other player did). Just two inches separated them, but Russell was faster and had the benefit of consistent coaching from Red Auerbach, one of the sport's all-time greatest coaches.

Fellow NBA player Bob Cousy once observed, "Russell had better speed and quickness, so he could always beat Chamberlain to the spot. He pushed him out a little further from the basket, forcing him to put the ball on the floor once or twice. We always felt Russell could handle him one-on-one."

In retrospect, one reason that the Celtics dominated the game for eight consecutive seasons was that Russell led a very talented team of players. The best the Warriors could offer was Chamberlain, and it wasn't until he was with more supportive teams that he could finally win a championship. In fact, Russell's eleven championships always rankled Chamberlain, who held two.

Basketball had its reputation tarnished in 1950 by an infamous point-shaving incident in college sports. It took the game years to recover,

The rivalry between Wilt Chamberlain *(left)* and Bill Russell *(right)* was almost always heated. The powerful centers often argued on the court and sometimes seemed to be on the verge of exchanging blows.

and it wasn't really until the Russell-Chamberlain rivalry caught sportswriters' imaginations that the game entered the spotlight. Just as baseball needed Babe Ruth to help recover from the notorious Black Sox scandal of 1919, basketball needed Wilt Chamberlain.

Russell's rivalry with Chamberlain also led him to develop his famous move, the fade-away jump shot, in which he took to the air, and, as he fell back, shot the ball over the heads of his opponents.

Fellow player Billy Cunningham observed, "You have to realize that the dunk as we know it—the scary power play it can be—started with Chamberlain. And the great defensive player, the man capable of stopping the dunk—was Russell. They are the two greatest talents to ever play the game. When you were on the court with them, they so dominated that you'd find yourself stopping just to watch them. I've never had that feeling with any two other players."

"What made it fun to watch those guys was that everyone knew there was no love between them," fellow player Wayne Embry recalled. "Off the court, they get along, but they wanted to defend each other more than anything in the world."

Referee Norm Drucker also noted that in the twenty-five match-ups he worked, neither player took a cheap shot at the other. They were professionals who played their game as well as they knew how.

The NBA's Unhappiest Rookie of the Year

Although the Warriors played well because of Chamberlain, they still came in second place, losing in the semifinals to the Celtics in six games. That took some of the glory out of an exciting debut year in which he was named NBA Rookie of the Year, All-Star Game Most Valuable Player (MVP), and NBA Most Valuable Player.

Hurt and frustrated with his coach and his teammates, Chamberlain stunned the sports world with word of his retirement after just one season in the big league. Although he thought that he was doing what was best for him, it ignited a firestorm of controversy, with most public opinion against his decision. Friends, teammates, rivals, and the media loudly blasted his announcement.

Wisely, Chamberlain spent the summer touring Europe with the Harlem Globetrotters, where he had a chance to reconsider. By September he reversed himself and re-signed for his second season.

Eddie Gottlieb, not wanting to lose his drawing card, replaced Coach Johnston with Frank McGuire. Interestingly, it was McGuire who coached the North Carolina team that had beaten Chamberlain and the Kansas City Jayhawks in the famous championship college match. The new coach immediately sat down with Chamberlain and the two reached an understanding. "Thank God for my second professional coach," Chamberlain wrote in his autobiography, "who respected my ability, but most of all treated me as an equal. He understood my volatile position in both basketball and society."

"One night, we were on the road. We had gotten lost; it was about two in the morning,"

McGuire recalled years later. "I had gotten a terrible hotel room and I was standing in the hall. Chamberlain saw me and asked what was wrong.

"I said, 'Look at this room, it's like a shoebox.'

"He grabbed my key, then gave me his key. 'I got a room twice this size at the end of the hall, coach. It's all yours.'

"Then he shut the door to my old room in my face, the point being that he didn't want any argument; he wanted me to take his room."

New Coach, New Agenda

McGuire's advice to the other players was simple: Pass the ball to Chamberlain and let things happen. Since the players were paid based on their statistics, most agreed only if McGuire would sit with them during contract negotiations so Gottlieb would know they were giving most of the scoring chances to just one man. This proved not to be a problem.

The Warriors did not win in Chamberlain's second season, but he was a much happier player and continued to entertain fans while posting amazing scoring records.

It was the 1961–1962 season that confirmed his place in the hearts and minds of fans around the world. Previously, he had been averaging 38 points per game, a new record, but that year he cranked it up and averaged more than 50 points per game. Within eight days, he scored 62 points per game on three separate occasions. Additionally, despite the game being only forty-eight minutes long, Chamberlain averaged more than forty-eight minutes on the court each game because of overtimes.

Every day seemed to bring something new and marvelous from Chamberlain. This included his personal best of making 61 percent of his foul shots. But nothing prepared either him or the fans for what happened next.

Chamberlain Makes Basketball History

On March 2, 1962, the Warriors played in Hershey, Pennsylvania, where they trained at the time. They opposed the New York Knicks, and the game was seen as routine. Chamberlain had stayed up late socializing the night before and was taking his time getting from his apartment in Manhattan to the arena in Hershey. Arriving three hours before game time, he took his time and played some arcade games. His scores were impressive, but no one saw that as an omen until later.

When the game started, everything seemed normal, with Chamberlain scoring basket after basket. But then people began to notice the score. Chamberlain was notorious for being a poor shot from the free throw line—except for that night. That was the night he made more free throws than ever before (28 of 32 attempts), forcing the score higher and higher. The Knicks were also playing well, so it was a high-scoring game right into the fourth quarter.

By then it became apparent that Chamberlain was destined for a career night. Frustrated by their losing score, and by Chamberlain's star performance, the Knicks began fouling other

Warriors, holding onto the ball, doing anything possible to keep it from Chamberlain. The Warriors, though, knew something great was developing and did everything they could to pass the ball to their star center.

The game was not seen on television either since basketball was then only usually featured in just one or two "Game of the Week" broadcasts. It wasn't even on the radio since neither team was headed for the playoffs. As a result, only a handful of newspaper reporters were present. Still, word began to spread that something memorable was happening in a town known more for its chocolate than its sports.

Chamberlain cracked the 70-point mark, and then, in the fourth quarter, passed 88 points. By this time, the fans were attuned to the game's history-in-the-making status. Possibly every person in the arena, except the five Knicks players on the court, wanted to see Chamberlain make it to 100 points.

When point 100 was scored, the floor was briefly mobbed. The final score was 169–147,

Chamberlain scores his 100th point of the night against the New York Knicks in Hershey, Pennsylvania, on March 2, 1962.

Warriors, marking a record not only for Chamberlain but also for the Knicks who achieved the highest score ever in a losing game. Chamberlain caught a ride home in a car filled with Knicks players and, as he tried to sleep, all he heard during the trip back to Manhattan was griping over the achievement. (It should be noted that although he played for Philadelphia, Chamberlain preferred living in New York City because of its more acceptable attitudes toward skin color and issues such as interracial dating.)

When looking back on the game, Chamberlain dismissed it as his career highlight, recalling only how exhausted he was by the end. "I'm prouder of my 50.4-point game average that season than of my 100-point game, because consistency did it," Chamberlain said. But, to the fans in the arena, that game was the stuff of dreams.

He told Jack Kiser of the *Philadelphia Daily News*, "I just don't want somebody to come up to me tomorrow and ask me when I'm going to score a 120 [point game]. Scoring 100 points once is enough for me. I never really

Wilt Chamberlain savors his historic 100-point explosion against the New York Knicks in the Philadelphia Warriors locker room on March 2, 1962.

thought I'd do it. I guess everyone else did, but I was never fool enough to believe anything like that." Interestingly, his historic feat did not merit the front page of that paper.

Chamberlain Changes the Rules

Chamberlain dominated the game so much that after his fifth season the NBA administration felt it was time to make some changes. With Chamberlain in mind, they changed the court specifications. They added four feet to the width of the foul lane. They also prevented players from scoring baskets from the baseline directly over the backboard. This was not the first time rules were changed because of a player, or because of Chamberlain.

In college, Chamberlain used to "stuff" the ball in the basket, regardless of who shot it. Officials decided the cylinder of space above the rim would be off-limits to players. After college ball adopted the rule, it wasn't long before the NBA followed suit.

Celebrity Status

Chamberlain was a celebrity who was constantly being asked to make public appearances. Over the years he adopted several charities as his own, such as Operation Smile International, a group that helps children born with facial birth defects, and the Sonny Hill Community Involvement League of Philadelphia. But Chamberlain was always there for his friends, family, and teammates, too. His attention to charity work stemmed from values that his parents had instilled in him. He had a strong sense of civic duty that he never forgot.

One of his early appearances was in support of former basketball star Maurice Stokes, one of the sport's first African American stars. Stokes's career was cut short after three seasons by encephalitis, a disease that causes inflammation of the brain and eventually paralysis. He could no longer play basketball or take care of himself. Teammate Jack Twyman and his family became Stokes's legal guardians, making sure he was looked after. Still, his medical costs were a problem. Later, teammates decided to host a charity basketball game at the famous Kutsher's Country Club, where Chamberlain was once a bellhop.

Twyman recalled about Chamberlain, "He was just out of Kansas University and playing with the Globetrotters, before his NBA career had started. He didn't know Stokes. The game was scheduled when the Globies were touring France. Chamberlain said not to worry, he would be there. In keeping with his promise, he took a

SPALDiNG
FOR SERVICE AND SALES
IN 1960
NEW
NEW
PROFESSIONAL
163

plane from Paris, France, to New York City, then chartered a helicopter to go to Kutsher's Country Club in the Catskills. He played in the game, took the helicopter back to New York City, and the plane back to Paris—both at his own expense. He was only twenty-one years of age at the time."

And he continued to play in that annual game for years afterward.

NBA player Wes Unseld recalled a banquet for the *Washington Post* in which Chamberlain made an appearance. It was his first emergence before the All-Star Game, held in Baltimore, Maryland. "He was Mr. Chamberlain to me then," Unseld told the newspaper. "I asked him if he would say hello to my mother. He went over to her and just charmed her to death. She was on cloud nine after that. After that, I always had a fondness for him as a person."

Despite the constant demands on his time, Chamberlain made himself available to fans right up until his death in 1999.

Wilt Chamberlain displays a Spalding basketball bearing his name at the 1962 Sporting Goods Fair in New York City.

Three Teams,
Two Championships

After the magical winning season, the Warriors followed the growing trend of relocating sports franchises to the West Coast. As a result, they became the Golden State Warriors during the 1962–1963 season. And because Coach McGuire did not accompany the team, everything felt new for Chamberlain all over again. "If I had him my fourteen years," Chamberlain said of McGuire, "I don't want to tell you how many championships we'd have won. Maybe we'd have won seven and Russell seven. I'm not guessing; I know for a fact. I'm not knocking Russell, he was sensational."

Once again he clashed with his new coach, Dolph Schayes. Chamberlain, who always did things bigger-than-life, blasted the coach in a series of articles run by *Sports Illustrated*, under his byline, but which were clearly ghost-written (written by another writer).

By then Chamberlain was wisely investing his huge salary and expanding his business interests into real estate, making him even wealthier. Given his athletic prowess and unique fame, he was one of the most easily recognized sports celebrities of the 1960s. As race issues continued to dominate the news, players such as Russell and Chamberlain demonstrated that they were the equals of any white athlete, bringing newfound respect to African Americans.

Chamberlain, an NBA Staple Sensation

Chamberlain led the NBA in scoring that season and the next, as more muscle and bulk were added to his already strong frame. He continued getting fouled quite a bit, but he

gained the reputation of not being a revenge seeker, letting the game play itself out. Rival Bill Russell told a Boston reporter, "He only had one flaw: He was a nice man. We'd beat up on him. He would never hurt anybody." Chamberlain never used either his size or strength to seek revenge. Fans often commented that he was "too nice," and should use his abilities against his adversaries.

Still, his weakness at the foul line was well known and was seen as his one Achilles' heel. Many teams used that weakness as a way to blunt his impact by forcing him to shoot free throws. He remained bitter about this obvious flaw in his game for the rest of his life.

This is not to say that Chamberlain always turned the other cheek. There are a few famous anecdotes that indicate he could behave with hostility. Teammate Billy Cunningham said the greatest play he ever saw was in 1967 as the Philadelphia 76ers played the Baltimore Bullets. Gus Johnson had managed a dunk right over Chamberlain's head earlier in the

Scoring came easy for Wilt Chamberlain, who averaged 50.4 points per game in 1962.

game, and once again Johnson had the ball. Chamberlain was between Johnson and the basket as Johnson was preparing to dunk once more. "Johnson cupped the ball and took off— he had a perfect angle for a slam. Chamberlain went up and with one hand he grabbed the ball—cleanly! Then, he took it and shoved it right back into Johnson, drilling him into the floor. He was flattened and they carried him out. It turned out that Johnson was the only player in NBA history to suffer a dislocated shoulder from a blocked shot."

Johnny "Red" Kerr has a similar story to tell. He received a broken toe when Chamberlain dunked the ball so hard that it hit him with amazing force. To avoid embarrassment, Kerr walked off the court and pretended to trip and injure his toe in the fall. Fortunately, occurrences such as these were few.

More often than not Chamberlain was a student of the game. He may have fouled out in college, but he never once fouled out in his professional career, one of the more significant—if less celebrated—statistics about him. Lee Jones, a former NBA referee, recalled, "My second year in the league and I'm in Phoenix for a game against the Lakers. We had a situation with Jerry West, who thought Neal Walk had given him a foul. It was the only game in which West was ever ejected.

"Chamberlain came over, looked down at me and said, 'Who do you think you are?' I mean, I'm thinking, 'What am I doing here?' But after that, we had a good relationship. Mendy Rudolph [another referee] said if Chamberlain complained about a call, chances are you blew it."

A Generosity Unmatched

He may have played hard, but he also lived life to its fullest, usually sharing his bounty with friends and teammates. He had a house built shortly after arriving on the West Coast, and when it was completed, he invited not only his fellow Warriors over, but also the entire Celtics team who were in town for several games.

Despite not having much fun as a Golden State Warrior, Chamberlain never let his mood affect the way he treated his teammates. When Nate Thurmond was a rookie, he said Chamberlain took him under his wing, teaching him not only about the game, but also about San Francisco. The star took him to celebrity parties and the San Francisco Jazz Festival.

Chamberlain never fully appreciated San Francisco, although he liked traveling the world and its many cities. But he was just as happy to find himself traded back east to the Philadelphia 76ers. Before leaving, he offered some advice to Thurmond. "When the Warriors traded him, and I was going to take his place at center, I was at his house," Thurmond said. "He asked me to walk around the block with him. He said, 'They aren't trading me because they think you're better than I am. Don't try to do what I do, do what you do best. Play your game. They're trading me because they don't want to pay me. Never forget, Nate, you may love this game, but it's also a business.'"

Sports journalists interview Wilt Chamberlain after the news of his being traded to the Philadelphia 76ers was released in 1965.

The Philadelphia 76ers

Just days after the 1965 All-Star Game, Chamberlain was traded from the Warriors to the newly founded Philadelphia 76ers for three players and $150,000. The Warriors' owner Franklin Mieuli said at the time that it was not easy to love Chamberlain. "I don't mean that I personally dislike him," he said. "He's a good friend of mine. But the fans in San Francisco never learned to love him. I guess most fans are for the little man, the underdog, and Chamberlain is neither. He's easy to hate, and we were the best draw in the NBA on the road when people came to see him lose."

Such feelings led Chamberlain to develop the lifelong opinion that fans saw him as Goliath, and that people always preferred David to the giant.

The new team was just starting to come together when Chamberlain returned to his hometown. Once he established himself, he helped the team reach the playoffs in the 1965–1966 season, only to lose again to Russell and the Celtics.

By the 1966–1967 season, Chamberlain was frustrated by not having won a championship despite his individual records, so he was ready to try anything. As a newly matured player, he took his redefined role very seriously. His total points dropped, but he led the league in assists the following season, easily earning his $180,000 salary.

Still, despite his defensive play, the 76ers lost once more to the Celtics. Afterward, Chamberlain began talking about a new contract, suggesting he replace soon departing coach Alex Hannum as a player/coach and even implying he be given partial ownership of the team. In those days, such demands seemed extravagant. The owner of the 76ers, Irv Kosloff, was worried that he could not handle the salary demands of arguably the most popular player in basketball.

But just one year later, the 76ers bolstered their team with the addition of Billy Cunningham, which put them in line to challenge the Celtics all season. The 76ers won forty-five of their first forty-nine games and found themselves challenging the Celtics for the championship. This time, Chamberlain got the best of Russell, and the 76ers became NBA champs. It was the first time a team other than the Celtics had won in eight years. In 1996, fans voted the 1966–1967 76ers the greatest team in all of NBA history.

One of the differences was in Chamberlain's playing style. Coach Hannum talked to him

Wilt Chamberlain (number 13) scores against Bill Russell (under basket) of the Boston Celtics in a regular-season NBA game on November 11, 1961.

about adjusting his game and being more of a team player. Rather than always receiving the ball for shots, he was asked to strengthen his defense and pass it more often.

The Los Angeles Lakers

Jack Kent Cooke, owner of the Los Angeles Lakers, was intrigued with Chamberlain. Like the 76ers and other teams, the Lakers were frustrated at losing to the Celtics year after year. Cooke felt he was a player or two away from building a team that could topple Boston at last. Cooke invited Chamberlain to his Bel Air, California, home, where the two men talked and sought a common ground. Cooke was very impressed with Chamberlain's depth of knowledge about things off the court. Chamberlain came away with the understanding that he would receive a $250,000-per-year contract for a span of five consecutive years if he would play for the Lakers.

All that remained was for Cooke and the 76ers to make the trade a reality. On July 8, 1968, Chamberlain returned to the West Coast, in exchange for Archie Clark, Darrell Imhoff, and Jerry Chambers. Sure enough, Chamberlain signed his very lucrative contract. He played his final five seasons with the Lakers, helping the team to reach the playoffs four times. He was paired with other greats, too, such as Jerry West, Elgin Baylor, and Gail Goodrich, and he wasn't expected to carry the entire team.

Coach Butch van Breda Kolff was less thrilled with the trade than either Cooke or the rest of the team. Talent scout Bill Bertka recalled, "Butch didn't have anything against Chamberlain or his effectiveness as a basketball player. But you had to have Chamberlain in the post, and that dictated a style of offense play that Butch didn't particularly like. He'd rather have all five men moving, [and] all five men in interchangeable positions sharing the ball."

Sure enough, friction developed between the veteran coach and the veteran superstar. At the annual Maurice Stokes Charity Basketball Game at Kutsher's Country Club, van Breda Kolff asked Chamberlain to wear a Lakers T-shirt

and pose with him for the press. Chamberlain, still stung from comments van Breda Kolff had made to the media, refused. This set the stage for a tense preseason for everyone on the Lakers.

Chamberlain played well for the team, adjusting his playing style as its needs changed—either leading the team in rebounding or leading them with assists. Coach van Breda Kolff seemed dismayed by Chamberlain's performance, thinking that he was slacking off and not giving the game his best effort. One night that season, Washington Bullets' rookie Wes Unseld outperformed Chamberlain and, as a result, van Breda Kolff benched his famous center.

The reporters and commentators made much of the tension between player and coach, and fans flocked to see the games. Attendance was up, and the fans warmed to Chamberlain.

Van Breda Kolff and Chamberlain disagreed about most everything, including where Chamberlain liked to play on the court. He'd usually position himself at the left low post to be ready for rebounds. That seemed to put him in Elgin Baylor's preferred

Los Angeles Lakers center Wilt Chamberlain powers home a dunk as his Boston Celtics opponents look on in dismay.

path, so van Breda Kolff wanted him higher and closer to the center. These disagreements may have affected the outcome of the overall game. Even sports critics who reported on that season's games noted that the style of play seemed slower.

As the fights between them grew more frequent and heated, management stepped in repeatedly to bring about a truce, which lasted only briefly. Chamberlain started taking his frustrations out on his teammates, which prompted team captain Baylor to have a players-only meeting to settle the team's overall concerns.

The Celtics-Lakers Series

Over the next several months, the situation started to correct itself and the Lakers played with renewed vigor. They improved so much, in fact, that they challenged the Celtics that year, fully expecting to beat them in the championship game. The resounding beating the Lakers gave the Celtics a week before the season ended was seen on national television and fueled expectations. Jerry West had never played on a championship team and desperately wanted a win, thinking Russell and the Celtics were an aging group who could be beaten.

The Lakers, too, were showing signs of age since Baylor, their mainstay player, was getting older. The Celtics-Lakers series was one of the best displays of basketball ever played, with the seasoned Lakers on the losing side. During the final match, with less than six minutes of game time remaining, Chamberlain injured his knee. As a result he asked to come off the court, and the Lakers struggled to maintain their lead. Legend has it that with three minutes left, Chamberlain asked to return, and Coach van Breda Kolff, preferring the moves of substitute player Mel Counts, refused to allow him to return. Chamberlain sat on the bench for the remainder of the game where he watched his team lose from the sidelines. His longtime rival, Bill Russell, was critical of Chamberlain's decision to leave the court after his injury. The team's loss and Chamberlain's decision ultimately hurt their friendship.

Coach van Breda Kolff resigned after that season and was replaced by Joe Mullaney, who immediately told the *Los Angeles Times*, "Chamberlain is a special player and must be treated in a special way." This opinion set a different tone for the entire team and made their star center a much happier athlete.

However, the 1969–1970 season was seen as a lost opportunity for the Lakers. Coach Mullaney had asked Chamberlain to increase his defensive skills to help the team and he was happy to oblige. But in less than ten games he hurt his knee and was effectively out for the remainder of the season. Despite declaring that he would be back to play, the Lakers had to make other plans. Captain Baylor also suffered a bittersweet season. He was getting older and his skills were on the decline. The previous year, with Chamberlain in the low-post position, Baylor altered his playing style and attempted more jump shots, which made him less effective. In 1970, he returned to form and played better, but he was also much slower, his impact eroded. This led to a decline in his authority as team captain, and, as a result, the Lakers' playing style also suffered.

During his rehabilitation, Chamberlain received a great deal of attention, prompting him to comment, "I've been surprised at the nice fan mail I've gotten since I've been hurt. I guess my injuries have made me seem human and have made people sympathize with me for the first time. Usually, I've been regarded as some kind of animal." The man who forever changed basketball still regarded himself as unpopular with fans of the sport.

Before this injury Chamberlain had missed only a dozen games in his career, so sitting out was a new, as well as uncomfortable experience. As a result, he worked diligently to recover and returned to the court in time for the final three games of the regular season. It heartened the team and the fans, but it wasn't enough to keep the Lakers from falling to the New York Knicks.

Hungry for a Championship

Throughout the history of the game, there have been many times when players came together and formed an indomitable force. The 76ers team of the mid-1960s was such a group, as were the Celtics throughout that entire decade. The Knicks of the early 1970s, the Celtics and its star Larry Bird of the late 1970s, and Michael Jordan and the Chicago Bulls of the 1990s were other noteworthy "dream teams." To Chamberlain, not being part of such a team meant his chances of another championship were fading fast. Russell was already retired for two years by 1971, and Chamberlain wondered how many more seasons he had left on the court. Had the opportunity for greatness passed him by? Such thoughts occupied his mind during the off-season, as they did Jerry West, who faced the end of his terrific career, too.

Cooke, the Lakers' owner, was also impatient for victory, so he replaced Coach Mullaney with Bill Sharman for the 1971–1972 season. Sharman had a career on both the collegiate and professional basketball level, but

Los Angeles Lakers coach Bill Sharman looks up at Chamberlain as he describes a play during a time-out in their game against the Cleveland Cavaliers on January 5, 1971.

had never handled a championship team. His friends said he would be more successful working with younger players on their way up, not a team with its stars fading. The owner said he liked Sharman's inner intensity, which was first on display during his playing days with the Celtics, and Cooke thought that his attitude would spark his players.

Sharman was a different kind of coach, one who prepared thoroughly for each game and helped players establish better habits. He was the first coach to drill his players on shooting each day before a game. He was also the first coach to study films of previous games, seeing which plays worked and where the team needed to train more aggressively. Sharman paid more attention to the players' diets, making sure they ate well and remained healthy.

That year the Lakers were home to veteran players such as Chamberlain, West, Baylor, and Goodrich, as well as rookies including Pat Riley and Keith Erickson. They had to alter their rhythms and relationships to conform to Sharman's different approach to coaching, but they accepted his intense work ethic and it made them a better prepared team for the new season.

Now a Team Captain

Chamberlain wasn't sure what to make of Sharman and his unorthodox approach to the game. The two went out for lunch early in the season and Sharman explained his philosophy, selling Chamberlain on the changes that he proposed. These changes included reshuffling players' positions and turning the Lakers into a team that would run the court, instead of just positioning themselves and shooting. Chamberlain wasn't certain about the new strategy, but agreed to try it. He also practiced his free throw and improved it markedly, although his progress never seemed to translate from practice trials to an actual game.

Sharman had many strong personalities to manage, and his toughest decision came after the first nine games of the season. The coach decided to sit out Baylor and start rookie Jim McMillan. Rather than take a reserve role, Baylor immediately announced his retirement. The revamped line-up sparked to life and the very next night the Lakers won the first of thirty-three straight decisions, a new record.

To date, their 69–13 record has withstood the test of history. "All the pieces just fit," Sharman said at the time.

Along the way, Chamberlain, who was named team captain after Baylor's retirement, seemed rejuvenated. Many of his opponents felt he was faster and stronger at age thirty-five than ever before. Even tipping the scales at 300 pounds, Chamberlain ran, passed, rebounded, and guarded with renewed vigor.

This new playing style was good for the team, but Chamberlain disliked seeing his average score dip to just below 15 points per game. To a skilled shooter like him, being asked to do all the other work was akin to homerun slugger Babe Ruth being asked to be a bunter.

By this time, the NBA had become established as the fourth major sports league, along with baseball, football, and hockey. Legendary Celtics coach Red Auerbach credited Chamberlain. "His dominance, and his rivalry with Bill Russell, said it all."

The Lakers' fastbreak running game got them to the playoffs with an enviable record. Their first competition was with the Chicago Bulls, who fell in just four games. For the

Western Division Finals they had stiffer competition from the Milwaukee Bucks, led by Kareem Abdul-Jabbar. It lasted for five games, but the Lakers prevailed. At one point in Game 3, Chamberlain managed to keep Jabbar from scoring during the game's final eleven minutes.

Another Injury, Another Championship

Once more, it was the Lakers versus the Knicks for the championship. Both teams were tired and were nursing injuries. The pundits were uncertain who would win but knew the games would be hard-fought battles. Sure enough, in Game 4 Chamberlain sprained his wrist, another injury that slowed down the tired ballplayer. He stayed in the game and picked up his fifth foul as the contest hit overtime. Chamberlain prided himself on never fouling out of a professional game—a player fouls out after being assessed six fouls— and people expected him to take it easy. Instead, he played just as powerfully as ever, and helped his team win with a final score of 116–111.

Taking medication for his injury, Chamberlain went out to the court for Game 5 and helped the Lakers get their deserved victory. This was two championships for Chamberlain; to make it sweeter for the veteran star, he was named Finals MVP for the second time.

The following year, the Lakers seemed to lack the same drive. Almost everyone predicted that they couldn't repeat their performance as NBA champs. However, the quiet season saw them attain a playoff berth. They moved past the Bulls once again, and then surprised many by beating the Golden State Warriors. Here they were, for the fourth time in Chamberlain's five-year tenure as a Laker, reaching the championships. Not surprisingly, their opponents were the New York Knicks.

The New Yorkers arrived in Los Angeles for the first game exhausted, having fought the Celtics for the eastern crown in seven tough contests. At first, the Lakers seemed like they might have the edge, but once the Knicks got a

Wilt Chamberlain of the Los Angeles Lakers fires up a scoop shot against the New York Knicks in their playoff game in Los Angeles on April 30, 1972.

little rest, they rebounded and beat them for the championship.

Nobody Dunks Like Wilt

In the locker room, Chamberlain took off his uniform top and a photographer caught the moment. It was the last time he would be seen as a Laker, although his retirement would not be official until September. The team played very well together, but the players were never personally close. Coach Sharman, who injured his voice with intense sideline screaming for two seasons, didn't have the strength to hold them together.

After the 1972–1973 season, Chamberlain retired. He went out in style, though, leading the league in rebounds and field goal percentages. Chamberlain was the preeminent basketball star after Russell retired, but there was a new generation on the horizon and he saw that the time had come to step aside.

Bob Ferry, who played for the St. Louis Hawks, the Detroit Pistons, and the Baltimore Bullets, remembered his opponent this way in the

Washington Post: "There is nobody who dunks like Wilt, so hard that many times the ball bounced off the floor and went back up and hit the rim. Not taking anything away from Bill Russell, but I wonder just how Wilt would be remembered if he had played with the genius [coaching] of Red Auerbach early in his career."

Long before his fourteen-year stint on the NBA, Chamberlain played for Auerbach as a teen at Kutsher's Country Club during the summer. The legendary coach had tried to woo him to the Boston area, but Chamberlain had stuck beside Ed Gottlieb instead. His loyalty demonstrated something about his character, but it also led to a series of unsatisfying relationships with other coaches that may have hindered his career, despite how well-regarded he remains.

6

Coach, Author, and Actor

For many star players, ending a long, record-breaking professional sports career is a difficult life change. Many, like Bill Sharman and Pat Riley, turned to coaching and went on to have respected second careers while still enjoying the game they loved.

Chamberlain accepted an offer to coach the American Basketball Association's (ABA) San Diego Conquistadors. He thought he might be a player/coach, but the NBA contended that he had a contract forbidding him from playing in a rival league. Chamberlain tried his best to coach the team but lacked experience working in this manner. If he had worked under one or two great coaches for any length of time, those experiences would have better prepared him.

He did use some of Coach Sharman's advice, though, such as shooting practice drills in the morning before games. However, unlike Sharman, an assistant coach conducted them, not Chamberlain. He continued to live in Bel Air and flew down for each game.

For the players, the arrangement took getting used to, as did the lifestyle of their millionaire coach. Gene Moore told *Newsday*, "Every day there seems to be a different movie star at practice. Andy Williams was here once, then Archie Moore came the next day. Wilt works out with us, but he frequently has to stop and talk to some young lady on the telephone. But the thing we're waiting for most is for him to have a team party at his house."

"I'm really serious about coaching," Chamberlain told *Newsday*, "When I had a bad game, or made a few mistakes as a player, I always felt relieved to get it out of my system. But when you're a coach and make bad decisions, it affects you so much more."

After awhile, it angered Chamberlain's team that he was never with them until game time. He now had firsthand experience in understanding what life was like for coaches who made game-time decisions in an effort to improve players' strategies off the court.

The players' dissent was mounting. In order to afford Chamberlain's three-year contract, which paid him $600,000 per year, the entire ABA chipped in funds. San Diego had hoped to build the franchise around Chamberlain and his status as a sports hero. They wanted to work with town officials to build a new stadium, but a bond issue didn't obtain the necessary voter approval and the ABA slumped.

Chamberlain was also lured to the ABA in hopes of forcing a lucrative merger with the NBA, but that also did not happen on the accelerated timetable for which ABA owners had hoped.

The Conquistadors had an average season, and Chamberlain disliked merely watching from the sidelines. Still in remarkable shape, he began exploring other forms of

Coach Wilt Chamberlain of the San Diego Conquistadors discusses a play with Billy Shepard during an ABA game in 1973.

athletics such as tennis, volleyball, golf, and even polo, excelling in just about all of them.

During the 1960s, when Muhammed Ali reigned as world heavyweight boxing champion, it was suggested that Chamberlain put on the gloves for an exhibition bout. When the two legends finally met, Ali uttered, "Timberrrr!" Chamberlain was intrigued with the idea of stepping into the ring, and began thinking about a training schedule. Discussing the matter with his dad, the senior Chamberlain had a single comment. He simply said that his son's time would be better spent practicing his free throws. A decade later, the issue was raised again, but Ali and Chamberlain never battled.

Chamberlain, Bigger Than Life

Chamberlain did not have to work, since his years of investing had helped him to accumulate a huge fortune. He continued to dabble in real estate but remained on the move. Vague about his complete portfolio, Chamberlain always seemed to have multiple deals in the making.

"We buy land throughout the world and we develop it for commercial uses," he told one *Philadelphia Daily News* reporter, "[such as] low-income projects with the government. We do some things with other governments. We have a project here [in southern California]. I look at different deals as they come along."

He became a part owner of a fledgling volleyball league and played on that team, too. Given his size and strength, it's little surprise that he quickly achieved world-class standing in yet another sport. For a time, he even thought about trying out for the U.S. Olympic volleyball team, although he never acted on the notion.

Volleyball became his next passion, and he gave athletic clinics to children on both coasts and promoted the sport at the Big Apple Games in New York and at the Los Angeles Olympics in 1984.

Chamberlain owned houses in Hawaii and Los Angeles, plus an apartment in New York City, so he could move around the country at will. He ultimately settled in Los

Angeles in his final years, but to many he never seemed to have roots anywhere. Jerry West best described him as a nomad. Still, Philadelphia proudly called Chamberlain their hometown athlete for the length of his entire career and beyond, never forgetting about the city kid who made it all the way to the NBA.

Similarly, despite actively dating during his adult life, he never married or had children. He admitted in his autobiography, *A View from Above*, that although there were a handful of women he could have married, things never worked out. "I'm still looking," he joked with a sports columnist not long before his death.

As with many athletes, Chamberlain dabbled in Hollywood, too, making his screen debut in the 1984 film, *Conan the Destroyer.* His character, Bombaata, squared off against Arnold Schwarzenegger's Conan, but Chamberlain did not receive much notice for anything other than his size. He complained about his costume

Chamberlain as Bombaata in *Conan the Destroyer*

weighing nearly ninety pounds and about how he seemed to scare the animals he had to work with, even his horse. Filmed in Mexico, the locals were the only ones not put off by his immense physique, with most thinking he could be a major movie star. The lackluster box office receipts and poor reviews revealed otherwise.

His final role was as a 1992 guest star on ABC's series *The Commish*. Acting no longer appealed to the aging athlete, and the long hours that went into making movies did not agree with his active lifestyle.

One thing is certain: Chamberlain disliked the subtle prejudice in Hollywood, noting in his autobiography that "people of color" comprised 38 percent of the moviegoing market, but most black roles were reserved for the "bad guys."

Still, he did play himself in as many as sixty television commercials, several of which won the Clio Award for excellence in advertising. His final Clio was for a Sharp Electronics advertisement. He prided himself on never endorsing a product in which he did not truly believe, a commitment which made him very selective.

He also tried his hand at writing and producing, including his work on *The Wilt Chamberlain Story*, which was completed after his death. Similarly, he wrote the *Grizzly Six*, filmed in Canada.

Back on the Court

Athletics and sports were never far from Chamberlain's attention, and he soon found himself back on the court or surrounded by former teammates. In 1978, during his first year of eligibility, Wilt Chamberlain was inducted into the Basketball Hall of Fame.

In 1991, the 76ers retired Chamberlain's number, thirteen, in a huge ceremony. "I've had many teachers," he said during the event, "many people that I've admired and wanted to be like. And I dreamed of the day that I could do some of the things that they did then. But I never dreamed of a night like tonight."

An advertising mural by the Staples Center, home of the Los Angeles Lakers, showcases the great centers of the team (from left to right): Wilt Chamberlain, Kareem Abdul-Jabbar, and Shaquille O'Neal.

In keeping with Chamberlain's interest in charities, 76ers owner Harold Katz made a presentation of checks totaling $100,000 to several of Chamberlain's favorite charities, including the Sonny Hill Community Involvement League of Philadelphia, the Special Olympics, and Operation Smile International. He was also given a gold necklace with 100 diamonds in it, commemorating his 100-point game against the New York Knicks and his shining career.

Toward the end of his life, Chamberlain remained active, continually challenging himself. He ran a Hawaii marathon and a fifty-mile race in Canada when he was in his sixties. The sport of basketball never lost its appeal for him, either. Stories constantly appeared in the press, almost from the day he retired, that some owner or another had tried to get him back on the court. He even toyed with becoming a part owner of the Toronto Raptors expansion franchise when it was founded in the 1990s, but decided against it.

To celebrate the NBA's fiftieth anniversary, experts were asked to name their top fifty NBA stars, all of whom were honored. Chamberlain easily made the list. In the book commemorating the event, *NBA at 50*, a photo shows the still-muscular Chamberlain without a hint of gray in his hair, pumping iron.

His Passing and His Impact

Chamberlain remained intellectually curious and physically active until his death in 1999. He had grown fascinated with automobiles and had even done some racing. He had also decided to build his own vehicle and, in doing so, had clocked six years of design time, tinkering here and there.

In his final weeks he had seemed ill, losing some fifty pounds, but nothing was ever diagnosed. On the morning of October 12, 1999, Wilton Norman Chamberlain had a heart attack and died in his sleep at his Bel Air home, a residence he called Ursa Major, the pun a reference to his old nickname, the Big Dipper.

Chamberlain, remembered not only as a great athlete, continuously touched the lives of his friends and family with his strong sense of personal ethics and pride. His sister, seen here, embraces the Rev. O.C. Smith at his memorial service in October 1999.

His sister Barbara, who acted as spokesperson for the family, said, "He was just a wonderful person. He comes off one way, but he is truly a family-oriented person, a person who loves his friends and [whose] friends loved him. He is a person that will always be one of our favorite, favorite people. Not only because he was a great basketball player, but he was a great son, a great brother, a great uncle, and he was just a nice, nice person."

Fans, current players, and former teammates were stunned by the sudden loss of a powerful figure who never seemed to slow down. The accolades that flowed from television, radio, and newspapers were testaments to his impact on the game of basketball, and on America's hearts.

Chamberlain's death reminded people of all he had accomplished. Syndicated sports columnist Tony Kornheiser wrote, "Wilt was the most dominant individual player in basketball history. Don't even mention Michael Jordan. Wilt Chamberlain was on another planet.

"He has the most points in a single game, 100—a mark nobody else has come within 26 points of; teams don't score 100 in today's NBA for heaven's sake."

"Growing up in South Central Pennsylvania in the 1960s, I had nothing but sports figures to base my opinions about African

The Los Angeles Lakers observe a moment of silence before the start of a game, in memory of Wilt Chamberlain.

Americans," David Roelecke, a fan in Maryland, wrote to the *Philadelphia Daily News*, "All I heard in my town was the usual hogwash that still persists today. I was enthralled by Chamberlain's playing style and when he spoke, all the ignorance I heard was dispelled. He gave me more than thrills and memories. Wilt Chamberlain gave me enlightenment."

"[My favorite memory was] attending the Bill Russell tribute in Boston held in May of

1999 and witnessing the respect that Chamberlain and Russell had for one another. The standing ovation the Boston fans gave to Chamberlain on that night was incredible," wrote Rhode Island fan Richard Cardarelli.

Denver Nuggets Coach Dan Issel recalled to the Associated Press, "As I grew up, Wilt the Stilt *was* the player. The things he was able to do! I guess one year they told him he couldn't make as much money as he wanted because he couldn't pass the ball, so he went out and led the league in assists. Watching Chamberlain, you always kind of got the idea he was just playing with people; that he was on cruise control and still ten times better than anybody else that was playing at that time."

Of course, the game of basketball has continued without him, but his legacy has been engraved on the sport. Many others may have contributed to shaping Dr. James Naismith's game, but, arguably, Chamberlain propelled the sport farther than anyone else before or since. His statistical accomplishments remain unchallenged, and his legacy remains an inspiration to youths across the globe.

More than his work on the court, his charitable efforts also speak of a man who gave from a selfless commitment to better the world. That too is a legacy he has left for other athletes to follow.

Chamberlain may have been a Goliath at seven feet one inch and 300 pounds, but that just seemed to mean there was more of him to give. He played hard, he lived hard, and he never seemed to stop and rest. His mind always sought new challenges. His passing left a void in the world of sports, but his accomplishments remain from which others may study, admire, and learn.

glossary

assist   A pass from one player to another that leads to a basket.

backboard   The six-foot-by-four-foot board that is fixed behind the basket rim, usually made of wood or Plexiglas.

basket   The hoop through which the ball must go for a player to score; a field goal.

center   Usually the tallest player on a team's starting unit; the player most responsible for plays closest to the basket, including rebounding, scoring, and shot blocking.

court   The playing space for a basketball game, measuring ninety-four feet long; also called the floor.

dunk   The act of slamming the ball through the basket.

elbow To use one's elbow to impede another player. It is a foul if there is actual contact and an automatic ejection if the elbow makes contact above the shoulder.

fadeaway A jump shot that has the player stepping away from the basket as he or she releases the ball toward it.

fast break A play that occurs when the offensive team captures a rebound or a loose ball and rushes up the court in an attempt to score before the other team is ready on defense.

field goal A successful attempt at scoring by shooting the ball through the basket during regular play. Field goals are worth two points each, except when made from beyond the three-point line, in which case they are worth three.

forward One of two players flanking the center, usually on offense. Forwards play close to the basket and must be good shooters and rebounders. They are usually taller than guards but shorter than centers.

foul An illegal move or contact as witnessed by the referee.

foul lane The area from the foul line to inside the two parallel lines that extend to the baseline at each end of the court.

foul out The ejection of a player from a game after he or she has been assessed six fouls.

foul shot An uncontested shot, worth one point, taken by a player who has been fouled. The number of shots depend on the situation of the foul.

guard One of two rear players on a team, usually shorter and quicker than the forwards and the center. Guards are responsible for advancing the ball up the court and shooting from long distance.

MVP Most valuable player, usually awarded at the All-Star Game and the NBA Finals.

NBA The National Basketball Association, founded in 1949. The NBA currently has twenty-nine teams in the United States and Canada.

pass A move from one player to another, which may or may not include the ball making a single bounce on the court.

point shaving An illegal practice where, by using it, teams win a game by fewer baskets than expected, beating the "spread" as predicted by oddsmakers; used for betting. A point-shaving scandal in 1950 involved thirty-two top players.

post A position near the goal. A low post has the player usually under either corner of the backboard, looking to make rebounds. High post is toward the foul line.

rebound To retrieve the ball as it comes from the rim or backboard, taking possession of it for either team.

rookie A player in his or her first professional season.

for more
information

ESPN.com
506 Second Avenue
Suite 2000
Seattle, WA 98104
Web site: http://www.espn.com

International Basketball Association
One Corporate Place
1501 42nd Street, Suite 371
West Des Moines, IA 50266
Web site: http://www.ibabasketball.com

Naismith Memorial Basketball Hall of Fame
1150 West Columbus Avenue
Springfield, MA 01105
(413) 781-6500
(877) 4HOOPLA (446-6752)

Web site: http://www.hoophall.com
http://www.basketballhalloffame.com

Web Sites

National Basketball Association (NBA)
http://www.nba.com

National College Athletic Association (NCAA)
http://www.ncaabasketball.net

Philly.com
http://www.sports.philly.com/special/wilt

The Sporting News
http:www.sportingnews.com

The Washington Post
http://www.washingtonpost.com

for further reading

Anderson, Dave. *The Story of Basketball.* New York: William Morrow & Co., 1997.

Chamberlain, Wilt. *A View from Above.* New York: Villard, 1991.

Frankl, Ron. *Wilt Chamberlain (Basketball Legends).* Boolan, PA: Chelsea House Publishers, 1995.

Hubbard, Jan, ed. *The Official NBA Encyclopedia.* 3rd. ed. New York: Doubleday, 2000.

Lazenby, Roland. *The Lakers: A Basketball Journey.* New York: St. Martin's Press, 1993.

Ominsky, Dave, and P. J. Harari. *Basketball Made Simple.* Manhattan Beach, CA: First Base Sports, 1998.

Vancil, Mark, ed. *The NBA at Fifty.* West Haven, CT: Park Lane Press, 1996.

index

About the Author

Robert Greenberger spends his days as director of publishing operations at Marvel Comics and his nights as a freelance writer of fiction and non-fiction. He has several short stories to his credit, as well as numerous *Star Trek* novels. His articles have covered topics ranging from celebrity interviews to historic essays. His great passion is baseball.

He makes his home in Connecticut with his wife, Deb, and children, Katie and Robbie.

Photo Credits

Cover © Bettmann/Corbis; pp. 4, 28 © *The Sporting News*/Archive by Getty Images; pp. 8, 25, 50 © Archive by Getty Images; pp. 12, 13, 19, 33, 45, 47, 78, 92–93, 97, 99 © AP/Wide World; pp. 16, 23, 36–37, 59, 66, 73 © Bettmann/Corbis; p. 54 © Ernest Sisto/New York Times Co./Archive by Getty Images; pp. 62–63 © John G. Zimmerman/Time Pix; p. 85 © *Indianapolis Star*/AP Wide World; p. 89 © The Everett Collection.

Series Design and Layout

Geri Giordano